TWO PLUS

Can you tell which two of these eight shapes will make four squares of equal size when one shape is placed over the other?

Hint on page 46

DOUBLE TROUBLE

Hint on page 46

Answer each description with one of

1. Bars on a xylophone

2. 1 yard short of the total yards on a football field

3. Offensive players on the field for a football team

4. 7 times the next prime number after 7

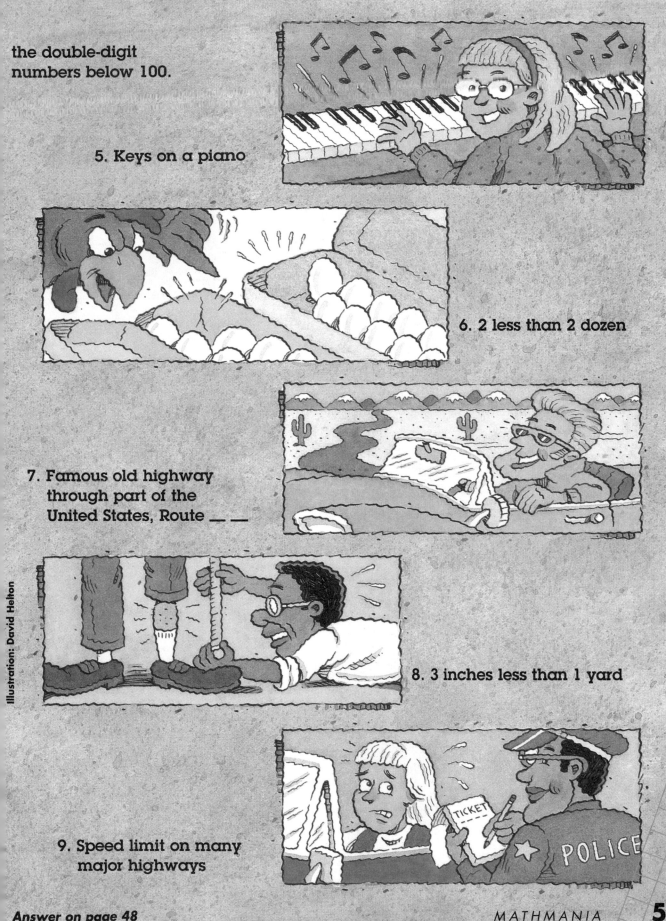

the double-digit
numbers below 100.

5. Keys on a piano

6. 2 less than 2 dozen

7. Famous old highway
through part of the
United States, Route _ _

8. 3 inches less than 1 yard

9. Speed limit on many
major highways

Illustration: David Helton

BOTTOM OUT

All the cubes below were formed by the figure on the left. Can you tell which letter is on the bottom in each case? The letters should spell out the answer to our riddle.

What occurs once in a century, twice in a lifetime, but not even once in a day?

_____ _____ _____

_____ _____ _____ _____ _____ _____

Illustration: Don Robison

Answer on page 48

6

CHANGE TEN

Belinda has 10 coins in her hand that total $1.00. The coins are not all dimes. Can you tell how many half-dollars, quarters, dimes, nickels, and pennies she has?

Illustration: Marc Nadel

Hint on page 46

Answer on page 48

E-MAIL EMILY

Emily has many friends. At the end of last week, she printed out the total number of

LAST WEEK'S E-MAIL MESSAGES	
Monday	
Tuesday	49
Wednesday	48
Thursday	96
Friday	99
Saturday	98
Sunday	42
	71

e-mail messages she received each day. Can you use the chart to answer the questions?

The day with the highest even number of messages was: _____.

The day with the third-highest even number of messages was: _____.

The day with twice as many messages as Tuesday was: _____.

The weekday with the most messages was: _____.

The day with the lowest even number of messages was: _____.

The day with only half as many messages as Friday was: _____.

The weekend day with the highest odd number of messages was: _____.

Answer on page 48

Illustration: Joe Boddy

EN-COUNT-ER

All the letters are given for this familiar statement, with one letter fitting into each blank. In the list on the left, all the letters following the 1 are the first letters of each word, though the letters are not given in the order of the words. The letters following the 2 are the second letters, and so on. Can you tell where each letter goes in each word? We've put three letters in to get you started.

1 — a a b c e h m s t t t t W
2 — e e e e h h I o o q r r r
3 — a e e e l l l n u u
4 — a a d f s t t
5 — e e h l t
6 — e s v
7 — d i
8 — d
9 — e
10 — n
11 — t

$$\underset{1\ 2}{\_\ \_}\quad \underset{1\ 2\ 3\ 4}{\overset{h}{\_}\ \_\ \_\ \_}\quad \underset{1\ 2\ 3\ 4\ 5}{\_\ \_\ \_\ \_\ \_}\quad \underset{1\ 2\ 3\ 4\ 5\ 6}{\_\ \_\ \_\ \_\ \_\ \_}$$

$$\underset{1\ 2}{\_\ \_}\quad \underset{1\ 2}{\_\ \_}\quad \underset{1\ 2\ 3\ 4}{\_\ \_\ \_\ \_}\text{-}\underset{5\ 6\ 7\ 8\ 9\ 10\ 11}{\_\ \_\ \_\ \_\ \_\ \_\ \_}\text{,}$$

$$\underset{1\ 2\ 3\ 4}{\_\ \_\ \_\ \_}\quad \underset{1\ 2\ 3}{\overset{l}{\_}\ \_\ \_}\quad \underset{1\ 2\ 3}{\_\ \_\ \_}\quad \underset{1\ 2\ 3}{\_\ \_\ \_}$$

$$\underset{1\ 2\ 3\ 4\ 5\ 6\ 7}{\_\ \_\ \_\ \_\ \_\ \_\ \_}\quad \underset{1\ 2\ 3\ 4\ 5}{\overset{q}{\_}\ \_\ \_\ \_\ \_}\ldots$$

Hint on page 46

Answer on page 48

Illustration: Bradley Clark

MATHMANIA

DOTS A LOT

Connect these dots in order, counting upward by 2s, to reveal a bumpy ride.

RAFTING RECORD

These adventurers are about to set off on a company rafting trip. Each raft holds four guests and one guide. Maritza, who is not going on the trip, is trying to keep a log of all the expenses so she can organize a similar trip next year. Can you help her keep track of everything and answer her questions?

Hint on page 46

Cost per person if raft is not full: $27.50
Cost per full raft: $105.00 (4 people)
Paddle rental: $4.50 ▪ Life jacket rental: $6.00

1. Total number of rafts needed for this group: _____
2. Total cost of the raft rental for this group: _____
3. Every guest is renting a paddle.
   Total number of paddles needed: _____
4. Total cost of the paddle rental for this group: _____
5. Katie, Kevin, and the Kline triplets brought their own life jackets. Total cost of the life jacket rental for the rest of the group: _____
6. Combined total of all charges for this group: _____
7. Total number of guides needed for this group: _____

Answer on page 48

ON AVERAGE

Last month, Ava took a test every week in each of four different subjects. Can you tell what her average is for each subject, based on her test scores?

Hint on page 46

SUBJECT	WEEK				AVERAGE
	1	2	3	4	
Math	100	96	98	94	
Language Arts	97	90	95	90	
Social Studies	99	93	96	92	
Science	97	98	99	98	

Answer on page 48

FAMOUS NAME

If you connect the dots in the order listed, you will find the name of the person described in this autobiography.

My name was *Lisa del Giocondo*. I was made famous in a portrait by an artist in Italy in the early 1500s. What people most remember about my portrait is my smile, which some say makes me look very mysterious.

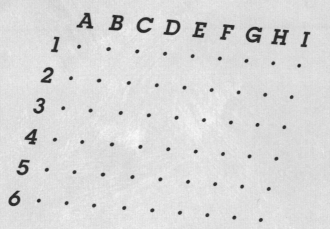

```
      A  B  C  D  E  F  G  H  I
  1 •  •  •  •  •  •  •  •  •
   2  •  •  •  •  •  •  •  •
  3 •  •  •  •  •  •  •  •  •
   4  •  •  •  •  •  •  •  •
  5 •  •  •  •  •  •  •  •  •
   6  •  •  •  •  •  •  •  •
```

D1-E1   H1-I1   D4-E4   D3-E3   A6-B6   D6-E6   H2-I2
D5-E5   F5-G5   A1-B2   F1-G3   B2-C1   G6-G4   F6-F4
E6-E5   D5-D4   C6-C4   A6-A4   I3-I1   H3-H1   G3-G1
F3-F1   E3-E1   D3-D1   C3-C1   A1-A3   F4-G4

Illustration: Kit Wray

WAY DOWN DEEP

The depths of some of the world's largest bodies of water are hidden in this grid. First add up the numbers for each sea or ocean. Each final answer will be the average depth in fathoms. Then swim over to the next page to find

BODY OF WATER	AVERAGE DEPTH (in fathoms)	
Pacific Ocean	2000 + 100 + 50 + 4	_____
Indian Ocean	2000 + 100	_____
Atlantic Ocean	1000 + 900 + 50 + 5	_____
Caribbean Sea	1000 + 400 + 8	_____
Sea of Japan	900 + 10 + 1	_____
Gulf of Mexico	800 + 80 + 3	_____
Mediterranean Sea	800 + 20 + 1	_____
Bering Sea	800 + 10 + 6	_____
South China Sea	800 + 0 + 0	_____
Black Sea	600 + 50 + 1	_____
Andaman Sea	600 + 10 + 1	_____
Arctic Ocean	500 + 60 + 8	_____
Sea of Okhotsk	500 + 30 + 2	_____
Gulf of California	300 + 90 + 6	_____
Red Sea	200 + 90 + 4	_____
East China Sea	100 + 3	_____

Answer on page 49

where the fathoms are hidden. Answers in the grid are hidden across, down, backward, or diagonally. Some numbers will appear in more than one answer, and all numbers will be used at least once.

```
3 9 6 2 1
8 2 1 1 6
8 1 9 5 5
5 0 4 4 6
3 0 3 0 1
2 8 5 6 8
```

Hint on page 46

Illustration: Michael Austin

GARDEN VARIETY

Mary, Mary, mathematician,
How does your garden grow?
With six numbered flowerpots
Planted in a triangle's rows.

Can you help Mary place these
potted plants so that each side
of the triangle has 12 flowers?

Hint on page 46

Illustration: Rick Geary

Answer on page 49

MULTIPLE MATCH

Multiple Matt likes to match up his answers to real-life objects. Do the multiplication on the left, then match the number to a definition on the right.

1. 3 × 1
2. 3 × 2
3. 3 × 3
4. 3 × 4
5. 3 × 5
6. 3 × 11
7. 3 × 22
8. 3 × 30
9. 3 × 44
10. 3 × 56
11. 3 × 120
12. 3 × 122

A. Strings on a regular guitar

B. Degrees in a circle

C. One degree above freezing on the Fahrenheit scale

D. Famous highway mentioned on page 5

E. Degrees in a right angle

F. Hours in a week

G. Colors on the flag of the United States, Italy, or France

H. Sides on a dodecagon

I. Days in a leap year

J. Number of player positions on a baseball team

K. Rooms in the White House

L. Minutes in $\frac{1}{4}$ of an hour

Answer on page 49

DIGIT DOES IT

Bob's Bow-tie Barn has been burglarized! But everyone's favorite investigator, Inspector Digit, is barely bamboozled. He's already at the scene and has found a hole. If you can help decipher the clue, Digit will be on the case at a good clip.

$\overline{22}\ \overline{6}\ \overline{17}\ \overline{15}$ $\overline{19}\ \overline{5}\ \overline{10}\ \overline{13}\ \overline{6}\ \overline{3}\ \overline{12}\ \overline{9}\ \overline{15}$ $\overline{22}\ \overline{19}\ \overline{11}\ \overline{19}\ \overline{12}$'

$\overline{9}\ \overline{5}\ \overline{3}\ \overline{6}$ $\overline{19}$ $\overline{12}\ \overline{19}\ \overline{6}$ $\overline{14}\ \overline{13}$, $\overline{10}\ \overline{9}\ \overline{16}\ \overline{6}$

$\overline{2}\ \overline{9}\ \overline{9}\ \overline{10}\ \overline{6}$ $\overline{6}\ \overline{5}\ \overline{22}\ \overline{10}$, $\overline{19}\ \overline{16}$

$\overline{2}\ \overline{6}\ \overline{17}\ \overline{7}\ \overline{19}\ \overline{5}\ \overline{11}$ $\overline{12}\ \overline{9}\ \overline{16}\ \overline{5}$. $\overline{19}\ \overline{16}$ "$\overline{20}\ \overline{5}\ \overline{9}\ \overline{12}$"

$\overline{10}\ \overline{12}\ \overline{19}\ \overline{3}\ \overline{20}\ \overline{19}\ \overline{5}\ \overline{11}$ $\overline{16}\ \overline{4}$ $\overline{5}\ \overline{6}\ \overline{3}\ \overline{20}$ $\overline{9}\ \overline{14}\ \overline{12}$

$\overline{17}\ \overline{5}\ \overline{4}$ $\overline{2}\ \overline{9}\ \overline{5}\ \overline{11}\ \overline{6}\ \overline{15}$. $\overline{19}\ \overline{21}$ $\overline{4}\ \overline{9}\ \overline{14}$

$\overline{21}\ \overline{19}\ \overline{5}\ \overline{22}$ $\overline{17}\ \overline{2}\ \overline{2}$ $\overline{12}\ \overline{1}\ \overline{6}$ $\overline{12}\ \overline{19}\ \overline{6}\ \overline{10}$

$\overline{19}$, $\overline{2}\ \overline{6}\ \overline{21}\ \overline{12}$, $\overline{4}\ \overline{9}\ \overline{14}\ \overline{2}\ \overline{2}$ $\overline{20}\ \overline{5}\ \overline{9}\ \overline{18}$

$\overline{19}\ \overline{16}$ $\overline{9}\ \overline{5}$ $\overline{12}\ \overline{1}\ \overline{6}$ $\overline{9}\ \overline{5}\ \overline{2}\ \overline{4}$

$\overline{12}\ \overline{15}\ \overline{17}\ \overline{5}\ \overline{10}\ \overline{13}\ \overline{9}\ \overline{15}\ \overline{12}\ \overline{17}\ \overline{12}\ \overline{19}\ \overline{9}\ \overline{5}$ $\overline{12}\ \overline{1}\ \overline{17}\ \overline{12}$

$\overline{15}\ \overline{14}\ \overline{5}\ \overline{10}$ $\overline{9}\ \overline{5}$ $\overline{12}\ \overline{19}\ \overline{6}\ \overline{10}$.

$\overline{22}\ \overline{19}\ \overline{3}\ \overline{20}\ \overline{19}\ \overline{6}$ $\overline{3}\ \overline{15}\ \overline{17}\ \overline{7}\ \overline{17}\ \overline{12}$

Hint on page 47

Illustration: Joe Boddy

SNORE SCORE

Three trolls live under this bridge. One big Billy Goat Gruff wants to cross the bridge, but he will do it only when all three trolls are asleep at the same time. Examine the trolls' sleep patterns, each of which repeats over and over, and see if you can figure out which hour it is now.

TUFF TROLL
Sleeps 1 hour
Awake 3 hours

RUFF TROLL
Sleeps 2 hours
Awake 1 hour

HUFF TROLL
Awake 1 hour
Sleeps 2 hours

	8:00 a.m.	9:00 a.m.	10:00 a.m.	11:00 a.m.	12:00 noon	1:00 p.m.	2:00 p.m.	3:00 p.m.	4:00 p.m.	5:00 p.m.	6:00 p.m.	7:00 p.m.	8:00 p.m.
Tuff Troll													
Ruff Troll													
Huff Troll													

Answer on page 49

22

CANINE LINES

Shep Boxer, the dog trainor for Bumbling Brothers' Circus, just set up the fences for his dog act. Can you help him move just four sections of fence to form three square pens to hold these canines?

Hint on page 47

Answer on page 49

Illustration: John Nez

23

SCRAMBLED PICTURE

Copy these mixed-up rectangles onto the next page to unscramble the scene.

A-3 A-2 A-1 A-4

B-2 B-4 B-3 B-1

C-4 C-1 C-3 C-2

D-3 D-2 D-4 D-1

The letters and numbers tell you where each rectangle belongs. We've done the first one, A-3, to start you off.

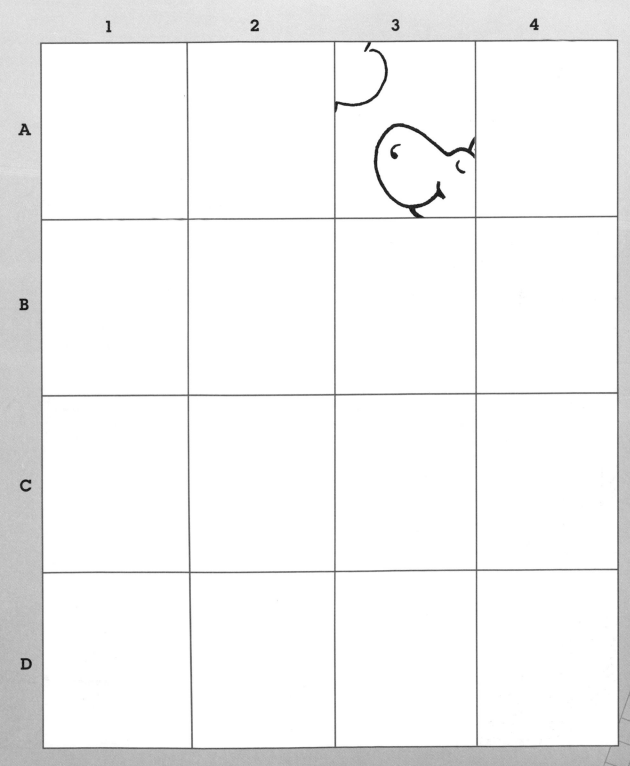

Illustration: Rob Sepanak

VIVA PIÑATA!

Rosaria has invited her friends to an old-fashioned Mexican fiesta this weekend. She wants to include some traditional piñatas as part of the festivities. How can she divide the candy evenly into the piñatas, with only the very smallest amounts left?

Lollipops
24 pieces

Mini Candy Bars
32 pieces

Sourballs
36 pieces

Sourballs
36 pieces

Sourballs
36 pieces

Lollipops
24 pieces

Bubble Gum
100 pieces

Caramels
30 pieces

Caramels
30 pieces

Caramels
30 pieces

Caramels
30 pieces

Illustration: R. Michael Palan

Answer on page 50

THE BIG SHOW

Tonight is the big celebrity show to benefit the local animal-rescue league. Check out the playbill and see if you can tell how many people are scheduled to perform.

Illustration: Ron Zalme

Act 1
The Bumbling Bambinis, a tricycling trio of acrobats

Act 2
The Magic Duo

Act 3
Minsky plus his musical quartet

Act 4
The Three Carltons

Act 5
Julie and Jules, the juggling jesters

Act 6
The Sizzling Septuplets on the high wire

Act 7
Verna and her dazzling dozen doves

Act 8
The Quintet Dancers

Act 9
Barbara Bigvoice and her orchestra of 100 horns

Answer on page 50

CROSSWORD RIDDLE

Fill in these boxes with the letters of the words that answer each clue or description. When you've completed the grid, rearrange the letters in the colored boxes to discover the answer to our riddle.

ACROSS

1. When facing a deadline, it's the _____ hour.
7. Prefix meaning "to do again"
8. Abbreviation for *Federal Housing Administration*
9. 3 in roman numerals
10. Word that ends a prayer
12. The two letters that follow Q in the alphabet
14. 51 in roman numerals
15. Inspector Digit deciphers this kind of message.
17. A perfect score in gymnastics
18. Short for *algebra*
20. Abbreviation for *North Carolina*
21. Last year for a teenager

DOWN

1. Having the same value
2. One of the Great Lakes
3. Carries blood through the body
4. Abbreviation for *not fine*, in comics and cards
5. Earth is the ____ planet from the sun.
6. Laughing sound
11. Latin prefix for 1000, as followed by *pede* or *meter*
13. A lucky number
15. One penny, or one ____
16. Less than twice
18. Half __ hour
19. Abbreviation for *gross national*, as with *product*

Answer on page 50

You can always count on these:

DIG THEM BONES

Last summer, Mugsy buried three bones in the backyard.

Illustration: Ron LeHew

To find bone number 1:
1. Start in A1.
2. Go east 3 squares.
3. Go south 2 squares.
4. Go northeast 2 squares.
5. Go south 3 squares.
6. Go southwest 1 square.
   Bone is in square: _____.

To find bone number 2:
1. Start at the spot where bone number 1 is located.
2. Go west 2 squares.
3. Go north 1 square.
4. Go east 2 squares.
5. Go northwest 2 squares.
6. Go south 1 square.
   Bone is in square: _____.

To find bone number 3:
1. Start at the spot where bone number 2 is located.
2. Go southeast 2 squares.
3. Go north 4 squares.
4. Go west 2 squares.
5. Go southeast 1 square.
6. Go southwest 2 squares.
   Bone is in square: _____.

Answer on page 50

Now he's trying to dig them up. You
can help him find them by following
the directions to each bone.

LIBRARY LAUGHS

Dewey has some funny books in his library. To check one out, solve each problem. Then go to the shelves to find the volume with the number that matches each answer. Put the matching letter in the blank beside each answer. Read down the letters you've filled in to find the title and author of the book Dewey just finished reading.

21 − 2 = _____

3 × 5 = _____

24 ÷ 2 = _____

18 + 4 = _____

3 × 3 = _____

28 ÷ 2 = _____

11 − 4 = _____

7 + 6 = _____

29 − 4 = _____

19 ÷ 1 = _____

4 × 5 = _____

8 − 3 = _____

6 × 3 = _____

5 + 4 = _____

15 ÷ 3 = _____

17 + 2 = _____

8 − 6 = _____

5 × 5 = _____

7 ÷ 7 = _____

7 × 2 = _____

7 + 2 = _____

28 − 8 = _____

7 − 6 = _____

7 + 4 = _____

4 × 3 = _____

35 ÷ 7 = _____

30 − 7 = _____

Illustration: Scott Peck

Answer on page 50

Hint on page 47

SAND ART

A real beach buff will be able to draw this figure without going back along or crossing over any lines.

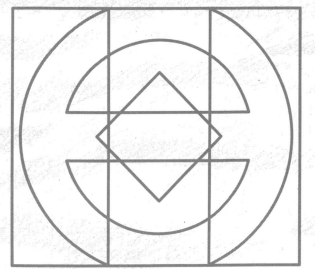

Illustration: Barbara Gray

Answer on page 50

STACKING STANLEY

Stanley has stacked the fruit aisle with some delicious combinations of fresh fruit. The price for each row of fruit, across, down, and diagonally, is shown on the labels.

$1.25
$1.45
$1.25
$1.10
$1.30
$1.20
$.90
$1.30
$.90
$1.00
$1.20
$.95
$.90
$.85
$1.10
$1.00

STAN

34

Answer on page 50

Can you help Stan mark the
price of each individual piece
of fruit? Stan knows that the
same fruit has the same price,
but no two different fruits
are the same price.

Hint
on
page
47

$2.40

$1.40

$1.60

$1.10

$2.40

$1.90

$3.00

$1.90

$2.25

$2.25

$1.85

$2.05

$2.05

$2.05

$2.45

$1.65

Illustration: R. Michael Palan

BEADWORK

Ruby is making beaded necklaces for her relatives. Can you help her figure out how much it will cost to make all the necklaces on her list?

Hint on page 47

Cousin Opal—Three dozen, less two beads
Aunt Pearl—8 more than Opal's
Aunt Emerald—6 more than Opal's
Mama Topaz—3 less than Emerald's
Cousin Sapphire—3 less than Pearl's

1 dozen beads = $4.35

Answer on page 50

Illustration: Rocky Fuller

COLOR BY SHAPES

Use the key to color the spaces and you'll see some new faces.

KEY

● —Blue   ◆ —White
▲ —Green ★ —Red
■ —Black x —Brown

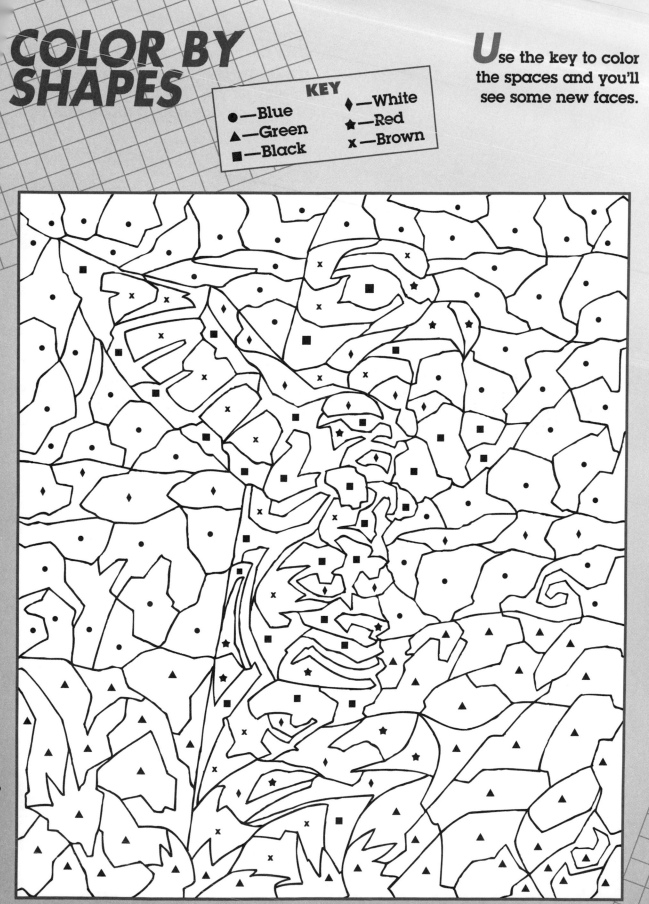

Answer on page 51

35

SEESAW SAME

The best buddy to have on the end of a seesaw is someone who is the same size as you. For instance, if $\frac{1}{2}$ were on one end of the teeter-totter,

A. $\frac{3}{4}$ — $\frac{25}{75}$ — 50

D. 3×3 — $\frac{18}{9}$ — 9

B. 1% — 10% — 1 — 10

E. $\frac{3}{3}$ — $6 \div 3$ — $9 \div 3$ — $\frac{1}{3}$

C. $\frac{3}{8}$ — $\frac{13}{48}$ — $\frac{15}{45}$ — $\frac{39}{88}$

Illustration: Don Robison

50% would be the perfect mate. Can you tell which of the three choices at each seesaw matches the number already seated?

H

16
4

4

8+8

20

F

9×2

72÷12

11-6

6

I

1/2

1/4

25

7/8

G

10

10

1%

66+66-140

18×18-8

J

8

88×8-696

Hint on page 47

MATHMAGIC

Let's do this one alone.

Choose a number with three different digits.

Reverse the exact order of the digits.

Write the difference between the two numbers.

Now reverse the exact order of the digits of this new answer.

Add these two last answers together.

Your answer is not that far away. It's right over on page 51.

Illustration: Marc Nadel

JUMP TO CONCLUSIONS

Brenda, Burgundy, and Brielle are playing the jump-rope game A, My Name Is Amy, in which each player gets one point for every letter completed. The list below shows each jumper's last completed letter for each turn. Can you figure out who won the game?

Hint on page 47

JUMPER	TURN 1	TURN 2	TURN 3	TURN 4
Brenda	J	M	P	L
Burgundy	Q	N	F	K O
Brielle	L	L	J	O

Illustration: Doug Cushman

Answer on page 51

PATTERN PUZZLE

*S*olve this puzzle in the same way you did "Crossword Riddle" on pages 28 and 29, except use numbers instead of letters.

ACROSS

1. 3666, 2555, 1644, _____, 422
3. 8909, 8918, _____, 8936
5. 505, 510, 508, _____, 511
7. 12346, 2346, _____, 46, 6
8. 3, 6, _____, 24, 48
9. 8765, 7654, 6543, _____
13. 11, 22, 33, _____, 55
14. 8, 11, 14, 17, _____
15. 10, 200, 3000, _____

DOWN

1. 9048, 9049, 9050, _____
2. 646, 535, 424, _____, 202
3. 54321, 65432, 76543, _____
4. 48, _____, 12, 6, 3
6. 01234, _____, 23456, 34567
10. 2, 4, 8, 16, _____
11. 125, 150, 175, _____
12. 25, 20, 15, _____
13. 80, 60, _____, 20

One digit goes in each box.
To get the answers, you have
to figure out the missing
number in each of the
given sequences.

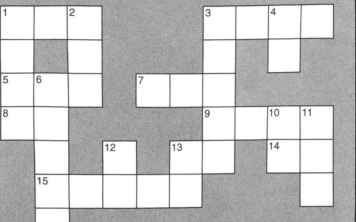

Answer on page 51

Hint on page 47

Illustration: Jim Paillot

IT'S A DEAL

Hint on page 47

Sixteen cards from a standard deck have been dealt as shown. The cards are jack, queen, king, and ace in each of the four suits. It's up to you to mark the face and suit of all 16 cards. The only rule is that no 2 cards of the same suit or the same face can be in any row or column. The same face card will appear diagonally in one direction, and the same non-face card will be in the opposite direction.

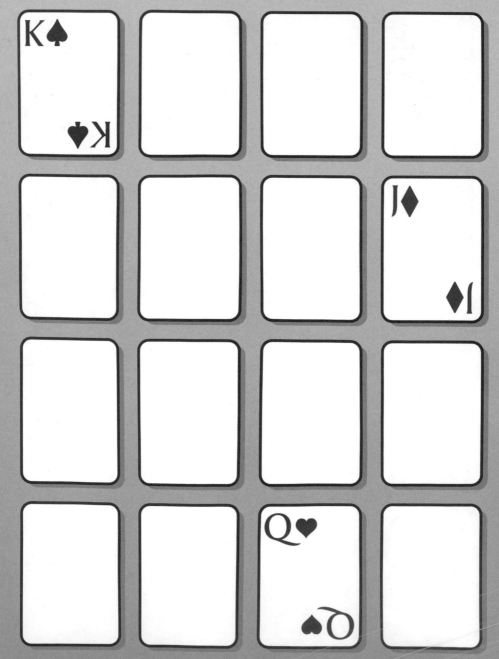

Answer on page 51

STAMP ACT

The three Letterman children have written letters to their pen pals. Now they want to divide the three sets of stamps so that they each have an equal value amount of stamps, even though they may not have the exact same number of stamps. Can you help them?

Answer on page 51

HINTS AND BRIGHT IDEAS

*T*hese hints may help with some of the trickier puzzles.

COVER
Every 12 inches equals 1 foot.

TWO PLUS (page 3)
Try to imagine what one shape might look like if it were placed over another shape.

DOUBLE TROUBLE (pages 4-5)
A prime number is a number that can be divided evenly only by 1 and that number. 1, 2, 3, 5, and 7 are prime numbers. 9 is not a prime number because it can be divided by 3 as well as by 1 and 9.

CHANGE TEN (page 7)
Belinda has at least one of each coin.

EN-COUNT-ER (page 10)
The answers become more evident if you start by filling in the blanks with higher numbers. All men will see that none of these words end with the letter *U* or *A*.

RAFTING RECORD (pages 12-13)
Don't count Maritza as part of this party.

ON AVERAGE (page 14)
To find the average in each subject, add up all four grades and then divide the total by 4 (the number of items you added together).

WAY DOWN DEEP (pages 16-17)
Be careful adding up the fathoms for the South China Sea. A fathom is a measurement of 6 feet in depth.

GARDEN VARIETY (page 18)
The flowerpot with 6 flowers will be on one of the corners. In our answer, it's at the top.

DIGIT DOES IT (pages 20-21)
The word *Inspector* appears in the note's greeting. Use the code numbers from this word to help figure out the rest of the message.

CANINE LINES (page 23)
The pens will be squares, but they will be different sizes.

CROSSWORD RIDDLE (pages 28-29)
You're in the right vein if you know LI is the roman numeral for 51. Milli is not just one girl in a thousand. She'd score a 10 in gymnastics.

LIBRARY LAUGHS (page 32)
Remember to consult the books to find the letter that matches each number.

STACKING STANLEY (pages 34-35)
If you find a row that has the same three fruits in it, divide the total price by 3 to get the price of one fruit.

BEADWORK (page 36)
There are 12 beads in a dozen. Find the total of all the beads needed, then figure out how many dozens are needed.

SEESAW SAME (pages 38-39)
1 is 1.0. Do all operations in order from left to right. .25 is the same as 25% or $\frac{1}{4}$.

JUMP TO CONCLUSIONS (page 41)
Count up from *A* to the letter given. For instance, the player who jumped to *J* scored 10 points. Add up the points for each turn to get the total.

PATTERN PUZZLE (pages 42-43)
1 Across is probably the toughest one to figure out. If you multiply the final digit in any number by the digit just before it, you will find all the digits before them. For example, for 3666, 6 × 6 = 36.

IT'S A DEAL (page 44)
It may help you to work with real cards to figure this one out.

ANSWERS

COVER
156 inches or 13 feet

TWO PLUS (page 3)

DOUBLE TROUBLE (pages 4-5)
1. 44   4. 77   7. 66
2. 99   5. 88   8. 33
3. 11   6. 22   9. 55

BOTTOM OUT (page 6)
What occurs once in a century, twice in
a lifetime, but not even once in a day?
THE LETTER E

CHANGE TEN (page 7)
1 half-dollar, 1 quarter, 1 dime, 2 nickels,
and 5 pennies

E-MAIL EMILY (pages 8-9)
The day with the highest even number of
    messages was: Friday.
The day with the third-highest even number
    of messages was: Tuesday.
The day with twice as many messages as
    Tuesday was: Wednesday.
The weekday with the most messages was:
    Thursday.
The day with the lowest even number of
    messages was: Saturday.
The day with only half as many messages
    as Friday was: Monday.
The weekend day with the highest odd
    number of messages was: Sunday.

EN-COUNT-ER (page 10)
"We hold these truths to be self-evident,
that all men are created equal. . . ."
This is the beginning of the second
paragraph of the Declaration of
Independence.

DOTS A LOT (page 11)

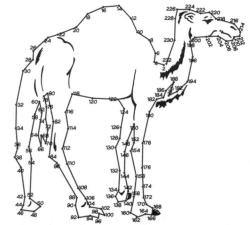

RAFTING RECORD (pages 12-13)
1. Total number of rafts needed for this
   group: 4 (4 guests in each of 3 rafts,
   and then 2 in the 4th raft)
2. Total cost of the raft rental for this
   group: $370.00 (3 × $105.00 = $315.00;
   2 × $27.50 = $55.00;
   $315.00 + $55.00 = $370.00)
3. Every guest is renting a paddle. Total
   number of paddles needed: 14
4. Total cost of the paddle rental for this
   group: $63.00 (14 × $4.50 = $63.00)
5. Katie, Kevin, and the Kline triplets
   brought their own life jackets. Total cost
   of the life jacket rental for the rest of the
   group: $54.00 (9 × $6.00 = $54.00)
6. Combined total of all charges for this
   group: $487.00
   ($370.00 + $63.00 + $54.00 = $487.00)
7. Total number of guides needed for this
   group: 4 (same as the number of rafts)

ON AVERAGE (page 14)
Math
   97 (100 + 96 + 98 + 94 = 388; 388 ÷ 4 = 97)
Language Arts
   93 (97 + 90 + 95 + 90 = 372; 372 ÷ 4 = 93)
Social Studies
   95 (99 + 93 + 96 + 92 = 380; 380 ÷ 4 = 95)
Science
   98 (97 + 98 + 99 + 98 = 392; 392 ÷ 4 = 98)

FAMOUS NAME (page 15)

The *Mona Lisa* was painted by Leonardo da Vinci.

WAY DOWN DEEP (pages 16-17)

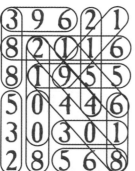

Pacific Ocean	2000 + 100 + 50 + 4 = 2154
Indian Ocean	2000 + 100 = 2100
Atlantic Ocean	1000 + 900 + 50 + 5 = 1955
Caribbean Sea	1000 + 400 + 8 = 1408
Sea of Japan	900 + 10 + 1 = 911
Gulf of Mexico	800 + 80 + 3 = 883
Mediterranean Sea	800 + 20 + 1 = 821
Bering Sea	800 + 10 + 6 = 816
South China Sea	800 + 0 + 0 = 800
Black Sea	600 + 50 + 1 = 651
Andaman Sea	600 + 10 + 1 = 611
Arctic Ocean	500 + 60 + 8 = 568
Sea of Okhotsk	500 + 30 + 2 = 532
Gulf of California	300 + 90 + 6 = 396
Red Sea	200 + 90 + 4 = 294
East China Sea	100 + 3 = 103

GARDEN VARIETY (page 18)

This is Mary's triangle. Your totals may be the same, but the pots may be placed on different sides of the triangle.

MULTIPLE MATCH (page 19)

1. 3—G	4. 12—H	7. 66—D	10. 168—F
2. 6—A	5. 15—L	8. 90—E	11. 360—B
3. 9—J	6. 33—C	9. 132—K	12. 366—I

DIGIT DOES IT (pages 20-21)

Dear Inspector Digit,
Once I tie up some loose ends, I'm leaving town. I'm "knot" sticking my neck out any longer. If you find all the ties I left, you'll know I'm on the only transportation that runs on ties.   Dickie Cravat

a-17	f-21	l-2	r-15	w-18
b-8	g-11	m-16	s-10	y-4
c-3	h-1	n-5	t-12	
d-22	i-19	o-9	u-14	
e-6	k-20	p-13	v-7	

Inspector Digit found 20 bow ties. He knew Cravat was in car number 20 of the train, which runs on railroad ties.

SNORE SCORE (page 22)

It must be between noon and 1 p.m. because all three trolls are sleeping.

	8:00 a.m.	9:00 a.m.	10:00 a.m.	11:00 a.m.	12:00 noon	1:00 p.m.	2:00 p.m.	3:00 p.m.	4:00 p.m.	5:00 p.m.	6:00 p.m.	7:00 p.m.	8:00 p.m.
Tuff Troll	X	O	O	O	X	O	O	O	X	O	O	O	
Ruff Troll	X	X	O	X	X	O	X	X	O	X	X	O	
Huff Troll	O	X	X	O	X	X	O	X	X	O	X	X	

CANINE LINES (page 23)

Here is our answer. You may have found another.

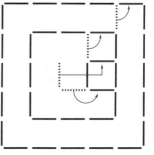

SCRAMBLED PICTURE (pages 24-25)

VIVA PIÑATA! (page 26)

Rosaria can fill each piñata with
10 mini candy bars (32 ÷ 3 = 10 remainder 2),
16 lollipops (24 × 2 = 48; 48 ÷ 3 = 16),
36 sourballs (36 × 3 = 108; 108 ÷ 3 = 36),
40 caramels (30 × 4 = 120; 120 ÷ 3 = 40), and
33 pieces of bubble gum (100 ÷ 3 = 33
   remainder 1).
2 candy bars and 1 piece of bubble gum
   are left.

THE BIG SHOW (page 27)

3 + 2 + 5 + 3 + 2 + 7 + 1 + 5 + 101 = 129 people

CROSSWORD RIDDLE (pages 28-29)

You can always count on these:
FINGERS AND TOES.

DIG THEM BONES (pages 30-31)

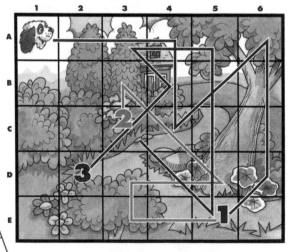

LIBRARY LAUGHS (page 32)

21 – 2 = 19	S	8 – 6 = 2	B
3 × 5 = 15	O	5 × 5 = 25	Y
24 ÷ 2 = 12	L	7 ÷ 7 = 1	A
18 + 4 = 22	V	7 × 2 = 14	N
3 × 3 = 9	I	7 + 2 = 9	I
28 ÷ 2 = 14	N	28 – 8 = 20	T
11 – 4 = 7	G	7 – 6 = 1	A
7 + 6 = 13	M	7 + 4 = 11	K
29 – 4 = 25	Y	4 × 3 = 12	L
19 ÷ 1 = 19	S	35 ÷ 7 = 5	E
4 × 5 = 20	T	30 – 7 = 23	W
8 – 3 = 5	E		
6 × 3 = 18	R		
5 + 4 = 9	I		
15 ÷ 3 = 5	E		
17 + 2 = 19	S		

SOLVING MYSTERIES
by Anita Klew

SAND ART (page 33)

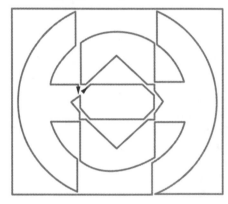

STACKING STANLEY (pages 34-35)

Kiwi:	$.20
Plum:	$.25
Pear:	$.30
Peach:	$.35
Banana:	$.40
Orange:	$.45
Apple:	$.50
Lemon:	$.55
Grapes:	$.70
Lime:	$.75
Cherries:	$.95
Strawberries:	$1.00

BEADWORK (page 36)

Opal needs 34 beads (36 – 2 = 34).
Pearl needs 42 beads (34 + 8 = 42).
Emerald needs 40 beads (34 + 6 = 40).
Topaz needs 37 beads (40 – 3 = 37).
Sapphire needs 39 beads (42 – 3 = 39).
34 + 42 + 40 + 37 + 39 = 192;
192 ÷ 12 = 16 dozen; 16 × $4.35 = $69.60